67582611R00083

Made in the USA
Columbia, SC
28 July 2019